COME SEE THE PLACE

COME SEE THE PLACE

The Holy Land Jesus Knew

Photographs by Gordon N. Converse

Text by Robert J. Bull and B. Cobbey Crisler

PRENTICE-HALL, INC., Englewood Cliffs, N.J.

Come See the Place: The Holy Land Jesus Knew
by Gordon N. Converse, Robert J. Bull and B. Cobbey Crisler

Copyright © 1978 by Gordon N. Converse for photographs;
by Robert J. Bull and B. Cobbey Crisler for text
Several of the photographs have appeared in *The Christian Science Monitor*
and are used with permission.
Art Direction and Design by Hal Siegel

Printed in the United States of America

Prentice-Hall International, Inc., London
Prentice-Hall of Australia, Pty. Ltd., Sydney
Prentice-Hall of Canada, Ltd., Toronto
Prentice-Hall of India Private Ltd., New Delhi
Prentice-Hall of Japan, Inc., Tokyo
Prentice-Hall of Southeast Asia Pte. Ltd., Singapore
Whitehall Books Limited, Wellington, New Zealand

10 9 8 7 6 5 4 3 2 1

Library of Congress Cataloging in Publication Data

Converse, Gordon N.
Come see the place.

1. Palestine—Description and travel—Views.
2. Jesus Christ—Biography.
3. Christian biography—Palestine.
I. Bull, Robert J.   II. Crisler, B. Cobbey,   III. Title.
DS108.5.C65   779'.9'2209   78-7054
ISBN 0-13-152538-7

ACKNOWLEDGMENTS

We are indebted to *The Christian Science Monitor,*
the American Schools of Oriental Research,
the Albright Institute of Archaeological Research in Jerusalem,
Drew University Institute for Archaeological Research, and the Daycroft School and the Israel Museum
for their encouragement and cooperation;
to Professor Benjamin Mazar, Dr. David Noel Freedman,
Mendl Nun, and those special few,
like Robert Hahn, Gene Permé, Hal Siegel and our
patient editor, Roy Winnick, who caught the
vision of this volume and have supported it along its way.
The Foundation for Biblical Research and
Preservation of Primitive Christianity of Charlestown,
New Hampshire, and the Charles Stewart Harding
Foundation of Flint, Michigan, through an ample combination
of vision and support, provided the travel and
research grants needed to obtain the photographs.
The foundation in Charlestown, in conjunction
with the Zion Research Foundation at Boston University,
funded the special Holy Land
acoustical project referred to in the text.

Jointly we acknowledge our continuing debt
to our wives, Shirley (Converse), Vivian (Bull), and Janet (Crisler),
for their constant inspiration and sacrifice.

G.N.C.
R.J.B.
B.C.C.

INTRODUCTION

Just as those who have seen Athens understand Greek history better, and just as those who have seen Troy understand the words of the poet Virgil, thus one will comprehend the Holy Scriptures with a clearer understanding who has seen the land of Judah with his own eyes.

Jerome

It was a chosen land—this Holy Land. Its rifts and hills and waters provided setting and symbol to those who walked there as patriarchs, prophets, poets, and teachers of men. It is a land in which humanity has expressed many of its noblest concepts, and to which it has often looked for hope and haven in extremity.

Yet the land of the Bible is not heaven on earth. Its very geography tests the human spirit. It is as if nature had compressed valley, desert, plateau, waterfall, hot spring, salt, mountain, wilderness, Galilee's living lake and the Sea called "Dead" into a narrow sliver of earth space, and then challenged men to carve their home from the superabundant rock.

Few man-made structures of the Biblical period have survived to our day, but until quite recently the Bible's natural backgrounds were largely unchanged. Now with the intrusion of modern civilization, its buildings and bulldozers, the Holy Land and its historic locales are inexorably altering.

Our objective in this book is to conduct you across the span of twenty centuries into the living landscape of the Gospels—perhaps to the greatest extent possible today, surely to a greater extent than will be possible tomorrow. To achieve this, we have walked the Holy Land seeking what remains of original sites and settings in an effort to preserve and illuminate Gospel history. We have avoided, wherever possible, the signs and structures of post-Gospel times.

Come with us then. Visit the scenes where Jesus lived and taught of mountain and mustard seed, rock and sand, thorn and thistle, wheat and tare, wind and wave. Whether you have visited the Holy Land in person or have searched it out through the Bible's pages alone, we hope this blend of Biblical texts, historical comments and photographed Gospel settings will provide you with a new perspective of an ancient land—the Holy Land Jesus knew.

Gordon N. Converse, Robert J. Bull, and B. Cobbey Crisler

There was in the days of Herod, the king of Judaea, a certain priest named Zacharias, of the course of Abia: and his wife was of the daughters of Aaron, and her name was Elisabeth . . . . And they had no child, because that Elisabeth was barren, and they both were now well stricken in years. . . . And there appeared unto him an angel of the Lord standing on the right side of the altar of incense. . . . .the angel said unto him, Fear not, Zacharias: for thy prayer is heard; and thy wife Elisabeth shall bear thee a son, and thou shalt call his name John. . . . And many of the children of Israel shall he turn to the Lord their God. (Luke 1:5, 7, 11, 13, 16)

HILL COUNTRY OF JUDAEA

The people of Judaea lived on a small, high, almost physically barren plateau. Geography gave them a strong defensive position with natural barriers on all sides: to the east, the Jordan Valley; to the south, the Negev Desert; to the west, the steep inclines which rise from the maritime plain; to the north, the deep ravines along the border with Samaria.

These sharply etched delineations define the central tableland of Judaea, so small in size that one can almost see its limits from a single central high place or cross it in two days' journey afoot. Here were separated, isolated, and molded the people of Judaea. This awkward little hill country became the homeland of "a people chosen of God," the platform of His prophets, and the site of His sanctuary. Zacharias sprang from that people and that tradition. He lived in the hill country of Judaea and served as a priest in the Temple at Jerusalem. It was to Zacharias and his wife, Elisabeth, in this already historic land, that a son was born who came to be known as John the Baptist.

And in the sixth month the angel Gabriel was sent from God unto a city of Galilee, named
Nazareth, to a virgin espoused to a man whose name was Joseph, of the house of David; and
the virgin's name was Mary. . . . And the angel said unto her, Fear not, Mary: for thou hast
found favour with God. And, behold, thou shalt conceive in thy womb, and bring forth a son,
and shalt call his name JESUS. He shall be great, and shall be called the Son of the Highest. . . .
(Luke 1:26–27, 30–32)

Now all this was done, that it might be fulfilled which was spoken of the Lord by the prophet,
saying, Behold, a virgin shall be with child, and shall bring forth a son, and they shall call
his name Emmanuel, which being interpreted is, God with us.   (Matthew 1:22–23, quoting Isaiah 7:14)

For with God nothing shall be impossible.   (Luke 1:37)

NAZARETH

The first mention of Nazareth in history is in the Gospel accounts. The town was apparently located within the ancient tribal territory of Zebulun. (See Matthew 4:13–16, quoting Isaiah 9:1–2). While the Old Testament mentions many towns of Galilee and while secular literature contemporary with the New Testament lists over a hundred villages from that geographical area, Nazareth is not among them.

On the other hand, archaeological evidence indicates that as early as the Iron Age, almost one thousand years before Christ, a small agricultural village did occupy the site of what is now Nazareth. Tombs of a type used by Jews from the late Hellenistic through the Roman periods (ca. 150 B.C.–A.D. 325) suggest that (even though not mentioned by literary sources) there was indeed at least a small Jewish community at Nazareth in the first century A.D.

That this community is not named in the lists of Jewish cities and villages given in Josephus' works and the Talmud may indicate that first-century Nazareth was deemed so small and insignificant a community that it did not merit a place in a list of villages in Galilee. Perhaps it was this rural small town's apparent insignificance that caused Nathanael to exclaim, in John 1:46, "Can there any good thing come out of Nazareth?"

And it came to pass in those days, that there went out a decree from Caesar Augustus, that all the world should be taxed. . . . And Joseph also went up from Galilee, out of the city of Nazareth, into Judaea, unto the city of David, which is called Bethlehem; (because he was of the house and lineage of David:) to be taxed with Mary his espoused wife, being great with child. And so it was, that, while they were there, the days were accomplished that she should be delivered. And she brought forth her firstborn son, and wrapped him in swaddling clothes, and laid him in a manger; because there was no room for them in the inn. (Luke 2:1, 4–7)

BETHLEHEM

Bethlehem rests on the slopes of limestone hills which are honeycombed with caves. For centuries, these have been used by inhabitants of the little town as living quarters, storage facilities, and sheepfolds.

The Gospel account indicates that Jesus was born in a manger. It was as early as the second century, however, that Justin Martyr, a native of Palestine, recorded that Jesus was born in a cave in Bethlehem of Judaea and then laid in a manger. By the early third century, Origen, who lived the last part of his life in Palestine, noted that a particular cave in Bethlehem was, in his day, pointed out as the place where Jesus was born. Origen lamented the fact that the clay manger originally found in the cave had been replaced by one made of silver. It was probably over this cave that Emperor Constantine, early in the fourth century, built a four-aisle basilica with its apse centered over the place where the manger lay. Above the remains of the Constantinian basilica now stands the larger fifty-columned basilica built by Emperor Justinian in the sixth century.

A later tradition records that when the Sassanian Persians invaded Palestine in A.D. 614, they destroyed every Christian sanctuary except the basilica at Bethlehem. For there the invaders saw depicted on its mosaics the Magi, dressed in Persian garb and bearing gifts to the Christ child.

And there were in the same country shepherds abiding in the field, keeping watch over their flock by night. . . . And the angel said unto them, Fear not: for, behold, I bring you good tidings of great joy, which shall be to all people. . . . And it came to pass, as the angels were gone away from them into heaven, the shepherds said one to another, Let us now go even unto Bethlehem, and see this thing which is come to pass, which the Lord hath made known unto us.
(Luke 2:8, 10, 15)

SHEPHERDS' FIELDS

The fields about Bethlehem (like those of the rest of the hill country of Judaea) are strewn with stones of all sizes. They lie amid long-eroded limestone outcroppings which jut from the sides of the low hills. In the cracks, crevices, ledges, and small valleys vegetation gathers—green after the winter rains; brown and parched in the summer's heat. Here and there small oak and olive trees grow amid the grass and shrubs. Water, at all times scarce, comes from winter rain, the morning dew, wells, and an occasional spring. There are no flowing streams.

The land, which could not sustain extensive agriculture or industry, did not produce a large city. Rather, the land of Judaea, best suited for the grazing of flocks, became the citadel of the shepherd. For generations shepherds have, like David, pastured their flocks in the fields below Bethlehem, wandering from patch to patch of vegetation and finding a fold for the sheep and shelter for themselves in the many caves that appear in the limestone ledges.

And when they were departed, behold, the angel of the Lord appeareth to Joseph in a dream,
saying, Arise, and take the young child and his mother, and flee into Egypt, and be thou there
until I bring thee word: for Herod will seek the young child to destroy him. . . . But when
Herod was dead, behold, an angel of the Lord appeareth in a dream to Joseph in Egypt, saying,
Arise, and take the young child and his mother, and go into the land of Israel: for they are dead
which sought the young child's life. (Matthew 2:13, 19–20)

HERODIUM

Starkly visible to the southeast of Bethlehem is Herodium, a symmetrical mountain with flattened top,
which can be viewed from either the hills of Jerusalem or those of Bethlehem. On top of the mountain are the
remains of a large, elaborate, circular palace-fortress. Built by Herod in the first century before Christ, it
was designed to serve as both the king's residence and a defensive position. To certain people living in
Bethlehem, Herodium would have been a constant and bitter reminder of the tyrant-king, who, in his old age,
had slaughtered the young male children of that town. To many residents of Jerusalem, however,
Herodium might have recalled the young king who had built anew the splendid Temple of the Jews.

When Herod died in Jericho, his elaborate funeral cortege including almost his entire army wound its
way to Herodium, where his body was interred. According to Josephus' first-century account, "There was a
bier all of gold, embroidered with precious stones, and a purple bed of various contexture, with the dead body
upon it, covered with purple; and a diadem was put upon his head, and a crown above it, and a sceptre
in his right hand . . ." (*Wars of the Jews,* Bk. I, Ch. xxxiii, 9). Archaeologists have yet to locate Herod's
burial place.

Now his parents went to Jerusalem every year at the feast of the passover. And when he was twelve years old, they went up to Jerusalem after the custom of the feast. And when they had fulfilled the days, as they returned, the child Jesus tarried behind in Jerusalem; and Joseph and his mother knew not of it. . . . And it came to pass, that after three days they found him in the temple, sitting in the midst of the doctors, both hearing them, and asking them questions. . . . And he said unto them, How is it that ye sought me? wist ye not that I must be about my Father's business? (Luke 2:41–43, 46, 49)

ENCOUNTER IN THE TEMPLE

According to the Old Testament accounts, the original temple in Jerusalem was envisioned by David but built by Solomon. This temple was destroyed in 586 B.C. by the Babylonian armies under Nebuchadnezzar, and the Israelites were carried into captivity. About seventy years later, the high priest Zerubbabel rebuilt the temple but it did not match the magnificence of Solomon's structure.

It was Herod who expanded the limits of the Temple Mount and enclosed the whole within a rectangle (twice as large as Trajan's later Roman Forum) of massive supporting walls. Only the lower courses of these walls may be seen and touched today.

Josephus described the exterior of the Herodian Temple proper as ". . . being covered on all sides with massive plates of gold; the sun was no sooner up than there radiated a flash so fiery that persons straining to look at it were compelled to avert their eyes, as from solar rays. To approaching strangers it appeared from a distance like a snow-clad mountain for all that was not overlaid with gold was of purest white" (*Wars of the Jews,* Bk. V, Ch. v, 6).

The model of Herod's Temple shown here is on the grounds of the Holyland Hotel outside Jerusalem and represents the building as it may have appeared to the boy Jesus. His discussion with the "doctors" or "rabbis" would probably have occurred to the left of the main temple structure. Mary would not have been able to venture beyond the "Court of Women" inside the balustrade seen in the foreground.

Now in the fifteenth year of the reign of Tiberius Caesar, Pontius Pilate being governor of Judaea. . . the word of God came unto John the son of Zacharias in the wilderness. (Luke 3:1, 2)

TIBERIUS AND PONTIUS PILATE

A battered stone, found by excavators in the steps of the rebuilt theater of Herod at Caesarea Maritima, has inscribed on its surface five lines in Latin. The middle line of the inscription can, without great difficulty, be reconstructed to read (PON)TIUS PILATU(S). This is the first known epigraphical evidence, apart from that found on coins, of Pontius Pilate, the governor of Judaea from A.D. 26 to 36. The complete inscription may have read "Pontius Pilate, the Prefect of Judaea, has dedicated to the people of Caesarea a temple in honor of Tiberius."

This inscribed stone originally would have had a prominent place in the wall of the temple dedicated to the ruling emperor, Tiberius (A.D. 14–37). The location of this building, called the Tiberieum, is, however, still unknown.

Literary evidence indicates that Pilate, like other Roman governors of Judaea in the period of the New Testament, made Caesarea, on the shore of the Mediterranean Sea, his principal city and the seat of his government.

Then cometh Jesus from Galilee to Jordan unto John, to be baptized of him. But John forbad him, saying, I have need to be baptized of thee, and comest thou to me? And Jesus answering said unto him, Suffer it to be so now: for thus it becometh us to fulfil all righteousness.
(Matthew 3:13–15)

And straightway coming up out of the water, he saw the heavens opened, and the Spirit like a dove descending upon him: and there came a voice from heaven, saying, Thou art my beloved Son, in whom I am well pleased.   (Mark 1: 10, 11)

THE JORDAN RIVER

The Jordan River comes from sources near the mountains of Lebanon and Syria (including the snows of Mount Hermon) and travels, often turbulently, to the sea of Galilee. When the river exits at the sea's southern side, it flows at first rapidly, then with diminishing speed, down the sixty-five-mile valley between the mountains of Samaria to the west and those of Gilead to the east. The lower Jordan, running amid arid wasteland, twists like a serpent before it empties its muddy waters into the northern end of the Dead Sea. Near the mouth of the river are natural fords where people, animals, and goods, even after the winter rains, can cross the hundred-foot-wide stream. Roads related to four ancient fords in the vicinity of Jericho have been discovered, and one of these led to ancient Ammon.

The precise spot at the Jordan River where John baptized is not known. If large numbers of people came from Jerusalem and Judaea to the Jordan, as the Gospel of Matthew records (Matthew 3:5), they would have come by way of the trade route which ran between Jerusalem and Ammon and which forded the river just east of Jericho. It is this part of the Jordan where the river slows its rush to the Dead Sea by broadening out into shallow and quiet pools and it is here that people could have entered its waters with ease and safety for baptism.

And Jesus being full of the Holy Ghost returned from Jordan, and was led by the Spirit into the wilderness. . . .   (Luke 4:1)

And he was there in the wilderness forty days, tempted of Satan; and was with the wild beasts; and the angels ministered unto him.   (Mark 1:13)

WILDERNESS OF JUDAEA

The Wilderness of Judaea extends over the lower eastern terrace of the hill country of Judaea down to the Dead Sea. Arid, barren, marginally supportive of life, it was the retreat of hermits, robbers, and the politically persecuted. Life there was lonely, quiet, shadeless, hot, and demanding. Here, in the course of less than half a day's walk, one can move from the noise and bustle of the marketplace in Jerusalem twelve miles east to a torrid, solitary, silent world where the very environment can be a threat to life.

And Jesus returned in the power of the Spirit into Galilee: and there went out a fame of him through all the region round about. And he taught in their synagogues, being glorified of all. (Luke 4:14, 15)

SEA OF GALILEE

There is a saying among the rabbis that "the Lord has created the seven seas, but the Sea of Gennesaret [Galilee] is His delight." This large and beautiful lake, shaped like an ancient harp (Hebrew *kinneret* or *chinnereth*), is nestled in the green hills of Galilee. Fish teem in its waters, and on its shores men have camped and settled and plant life has flourished almost continuously since Paleolithic times. In fact, stone tools and a camp with the skeletal remains of Galilee man, found on the southern shore of the lake, are evidence of one of the oldest human habitations ever found in the Middle East. By the period of the New Testament, Josephus could write that every inch of soil around the lake was cultivated and that the towns there were thickly distributed and the villages densely populated. It was among these towns and villages, in this pleasant valley and beside this lake, that Jesus moved for the greater part of his ministry.

And it came to pass, that, as the people pressed upon him to hear the word of God, he stood by the lake of Gennesaret, and saw two ships standing by the lake: but the fishermen were gone out of them, and were washing their nets. (Luke 5:1–2)

FISHING BOATS

Fish bones and fishhooks found in excavated sites around the Sea of Galilee indicate that from prehistoric times the forty varieties of fish found in the waters of Galilee attracted fishing settlements to its shores. The Talmud and the New Testament both note that fishermen were found living around the lake in the late Hellenistic and Roman periods. Dried fish from the Sea of Galilee were exported to Rome and other parts of the Roman world during and after the time of Jesus.

At least seven and perhaps nine of Jesus' disciples were fishermen, and there were probably more among his wider group of followers.

And in the synagogue there was a man, which had a spirit of an unclean devil, and cried out with a loud voice, saying, Let us alone; what have we to do with thee, thou Jesus of Nazareth? art thou come to destroy us? . . . And Jesus rebuked him, saying, Hold thy peace, and come out of him. And when the devil had thrown him in the midst, he came out of him, and hurt him not.
(Luke 4:33–35)

SYNAGOGUE AT CAPERNAUM

Of the visible ruins at Capernaum, the most striking is a synagogue of the late Roman period, beneath whose southwest corner there is evidence of an older structure having the same general orientation as the synagogue above it. The large carefully shaped and fitted native black basalt blocks of the lower structure are, it is thought, the remains of an earlier synagogue, possibly the very one in which Jesus taught (Mark 1:21) and, perhaps, the same one built by the centurion mentioned in Luke 7:5. The photograph shows a course of these black stones.

The limestone basilica above them was built facing south in order that its three entrances would look out on the Sea of Galilee and, at the same time, allow the congregation to worship in the direction of Jerusalem. The white limestone forming the late-Corinthian columns and the richly sculptured walls of the rectangular structure, now turned a golden brown by long exposure to the elements, is not native to the area. This limestone was quarried four miles outside of Capernaum and is in sharp contrast, both in color and in texture, to the black basalt rock which abounds at Capernaum. Two inscriptions have been preserved on two stone columns, each recording the name of the contributor of that column to the building of the synagogue. One inscription is in Greek, the other in Aramaic, and the names inscribed are as common in the region of that time as they are familiar to modern readers of the Bible. The Aramaic inscription is translated, in part, "Alphaeus, the son of Zebedee, the son of John, made this column." All three names appear as well in the list of apostles given in Mark 3:13–18.

And forthwith, when they were come out of the synagogue, they entered into the house of Simon and Andrew, with James and John. But Simon's wife's mother lay sick of a fever, and anon they tell him of her. And he came and took her by the hand, and lifted her up; and immediately the fever left her, and she ministered unto them. (Mark 1:29–31)

Now when the sun was setting, all they that had any sick with divers diseases brought them unto him; and he laid his hands on every one of them, and healed them. (Luke 4:40)

And all the city was gathered together at the door. (Mark 1:33)

THE HOUSE OF SIMON AND ANDREW

The house of Simon and Andrew in Capernaum was long ago covered by subsequent building and rebuilding, but its location may now be known and some parts of its walls may still stand. The clue to its whereabouts is in a travel account written in the fourth century after Christ by the pilgrim Aetheria, who, visiting Capernaum, saw what was identified to her as the house of Simon Peter and his brother, Andrew. Some of its walls were standing and apparently had been incorporated into a church.

In the present century, Italian excavators at Capernaum have uncovered a large octagonal structure which has been identified as the center of a fifth century A.D. Byzantine church. Under the center of the octagon were found the remains of ornamented rooms which had been used as a center for Christian worship sometime between the second and fourth centuries. Because of their location under the Byzantine church and in light of ancient graffiti scratched on the plaster of its walls, the excavators judged that the rooms found were the very ones Aetheria had seen; in their judgment the house of Peter had been found. If they are correct, the house lies on a street very near to and just south of the synagogue at Capernaum. Aetheria, visiting the house of Peter, could not but have seen the nearby entrance of the earlier synagogue, oriented as in the photograph.

And in the morning, rising up a great while before day, he went out, and departed into a solitary place, and there prayed. And Simon and they that were with him followed after him. And when they had found him, they said unto him, All men seek for thee. (Mark 1:35–37)

SOLITARY PLACE AT DAWN

Unlike the solitary places which Jesus sought in the Wilderness of Judaea earlier in his ministry, any quiet place he found on the west bank of the Sea of Galilee would have been green, full of life, cool, and lapped by water pure enough to drink. He would have seen dawn break over the mountains of Gilead and morning light first illumine the water near the western shore, then progress across the whole of the sea until at last the details of the eastern shore became visible. The solitary kingfisher seen here pauses in one of those morning moments Jesus himself must have experienced many times.

And seeing the multitudes, he went up into a mountain: and when he was set, his disciples came unto him: and he opened his mouth, and taught them, saying . . . (Matthew 5:1–2)

MOUNT OF BEATITUDES

Although it is neither so named in Matthew's Gospel nor its precise location given, one of the higher hills on the northwestern shore of the Sea of Galilee has long been called the Mount of Beatitudes. The sequence of events in the Gospel indicates that the mountain was near the Sea of Galilee and not far from Capernaum. In the fourth century after the birth of Christ, a traveler wrote that the hill where Jesus taught the Beatitudes was above a field where seven springs of water gushed forth.

Today there may be found copious springs just north of the town of et-Tabghah—an Arabic name thought to be a corruption of the Greek word *heptapegon,* meaning "seven springs"—and beside the Sea of Galilee. It is on this slender evidence that the hill above these springs and in the vicinity of Capernaum has been called the Mount of Beatitudes.

Ye are the light of the world. A city that is set on an hill cannot be hid. (Matthew 5:14)

CITY ON AN HILL

Almost all the cities of Palestine were built on hills for reasons of security. They could thus be seen from a great distance by friend and foe alike.

Therefore I say unto you, Take no thought for your life, what ye shall eat, or what ye shall drink . . . Behold the fowls of the air: for they sow not, neither do they reap, nor gather into barns; yet your heavenly Father feedeth them. Are ye not much better than they? (Matthew 6:25, 26)

FOWLS OF THE AIR

If we base our estimate on the number of different birds found in Israel today, Jesus could have been thinking of any of 350 different species when he spoke of the "fowls of the air." Both the Old and the New Testaments refer to birds mainly in general terms. Fewer than 20 different species can be readily identified from their Biblical descriptions.

Many bird bones, especially those of small passerine birds (that is, perching birds such as sparrows, finches, and larks), have been found in diverse archaeological sites. This indicates that small field birds were as common here then, and as widely distributed, as they are now.

And why take ye thought for raiment? Consider the lilies of the field, how they grow; they toil not, neither do they spin: and yet I say unto you, That even Solomon in all his glory was not arrayed like one of these. Wherefore, if God so clothe the grass of the field, which to day is, and to morrow is cast into the oven, shall he not much more clothe you, O ye of little faith?
(Matthew 6:28–30)

LILIES OF THE FIELD

After the spring rains, the hills and valleys of Galilee, Samaria, and Judaea burst forth in a profusion of daisies (seen here), poppies, anemones, and other blooms whose color and density transform the landscape as far as the eye can see. Because they are so widespread, are of such striking color, and grow in such abundance, it has been assumed that these are the lilies of the field which are referred to in the Gospels.

Now when Jesus saw great multitudes about him, he gave commandment to depart unto the other side. . . . .And when he was come to the other side into the country of the Gergesenes (Matthew 8:18, 28) *. . immediately there met him out of the tombs a man with an unclean spirit. . . . neither could any man tame him.* (Mark 5 :2, 4)

And there was there an herd of many swine feeding on the mountain. . . . (Luke 8:32)
So the devils besought him, saying, If thou cast us out, suffer us to go away into the herd of swine. (Matthew 8:31)

And the unclean spirits went out, and entered into the swine: and the herd ran violently down a steep place into the sea, (they were about two thousand;) and were choked in the sea. And they that fed the swine fled, and told it in the city, and in the country. . . . And they come to Jesus, and see him that was possessed with the devil, and had the legion, sitting, and clothed, and in his right mind. . . . (Mark 5:13–15)

A STEEP PLACE

The location of the country of the Gergesenes is not known except that it was on the eastern shore of the Sea of Galilee. There is some slight, and very late, indication that Gergesa can be identified with the ruins found today at Kersa on the eastern shore of the sea and at a point where the mountains of Gilead drop sharply into the sea. A tenth-century history of the churches of Palestine indicates that the church at Kersa, or Kursi, east of the Sea of Tiberias (the Sea of Galilee), was the place where the demon-possessed man (or men, as in Matthew 8:28) was healed. The remains of a large Byzantine church have recently been uncovered at Kersa.

And he entered into a ship, and passed over, and came into his own city. . . . And as Jesus passed forth from thence, he saw a man, named Matthew, sitting at the receipt of custom: and he saith unto him, Follow me. And he arose, and followed him.   (Matthew 9:1, 9)

CAPERNAUM SHORE

As an occupying power, the Roman government reserved for itself the right to collect taxes from the peoples of the lands it conquered. In Palestine, however, the collection of tolls for the transportation of property was an exception to the general rule. There the collecting of customs duties was left in private hands and the license to collect customs was sold to the highest bidder. As a result of this practice, natives who contracted with Rome to collect transportation taxes from their countrymen became at once rich and hated. Called publicans, they were equated in the minds of their countrymen with robbers and sinners, and the rabbis debated whether or not a Jew who was a tax collector could ever be forgiven his transgressions.

The third-century synagogue seen here from the Sea of Galilee marks the site of ancient Capernaum. Jesus probably disembarked nearby.

And he began again to teach by the sea side: and there was gathered unto him a great multitude, so that he entered into a ship, and sat in the sea; and the whole multitude was by the sea on the land. And he taught them many things by parables, and said unto them in his doctrine, Hearken. . . . (Mark 4:1–3)

A SEASIDE AMPHITHEATER

Where did Jesus teach "by the sea side"? No one can be certain. Matthew apparently pinpoints the Capernaum area, since his account opens with Jesus coming "out of the house" (13:1) and closes when he "went into the house" (13:36). This house has often been identified with the house of Simon and Andrew at Capernaum. But a major question to be raised is that of acoustics: How could one have been heard by "a great multitude" without the benefit of some sort of voice amplification? And is it possible to find a seashore spot with acoustical properties that would produce such amplification?

Among several coves near Capernaum, there is one that has recently been found to have just such sound characteristics of a natural amphitheater. Acoustical tests have been carried out on this site that show that "a great multitude" of some five thousand to seven thousand people, assembling here, could indeed have both seen and clearly heard a person speaking from a boat located at a spot near the cove's center.

Matthew reports that Jesus delivered four parables from this boat-pulpit, and three Gospels agree that one of these was the parable of the sower, the most sound-oriented of all Jesus' parables. In Mark's account Jesus' first word is "Hearken" or *Akouete* (a Greek word from whose root comes our word "acoustics"). And within the twenty-three verses that constitute Matthew's transcription of this parable, the word for "ears" and various forms of the verb "to hear" occur no fewer than twenty-one times.

Another parable put he forth unto them, saying, The kingdom of heaven is likened unto a man which sowed good seed in his field: . . . But when the blade was sprung up, and brought forth fruit, then appeared the tares also. . . . The servants said unto him, Wilt thou then that we go and gather them up? But he said, Nay; lest while ye gather up the tares, ye root up also the wheat with them. Let both grow together until the harvest: and in the time of harvest I will say to the reapers, Gather ye together first the tares, and bind them in bundles to burn them: but gather the wheat into my barn. (Matthew 13:24, 26, 28–30)

WHEAT AND TARES

One of the marks of a fertile field in Galilee, Samaria, and Judaea is the size of the stone fence which surrounds it. In order to enhance the productivity of a fertile field, a farmer will, as his fathers did before him, lift and carry the stones encountered in the field to its borders and there build a fence or wall. Thus the height and width of a stone fence around a field becomes a clue to the quality of the field. Good ground is patiently cleared, while poor ground tends to be left stone-strewn or fallow and fenceless.

Tares, probably to be identified with the weed darnel (*Lolium temulentum*), grow and develop alongside wheat, and as the young tares cannot readily be distinguished from young wheat, they both mature together. As wheat and tares ripen, however, the difference in their fruit becomes apparent. The farmer thus faces a triple dilemma: First, if he waits until his wheat and tares mature, the roots of both will be entangled, and pulling up the tares will endanger the wheat. Second, if he harvests both together, the milled tares will spoil the flour and bread in which they are present. Third, if he allows the tares in his field to drop their seed, he encourages a greater unwanted crop of tares next season. The only course left is patiently and laboriously to gather the mature tares separately and burn them, after which the pure wheat can safely be harvested and ground into flour. Seed grain saved from harvest for next year's sowing will now be free from contaminating tares.

Another parable put he forth unto them, saying, The kingdom of heaven is like to a grain of
mustard seed, which a man took, and sowed in his field: which indeed is the least of all seeds:
but when it is grown, it is the greatest among herbs, and becometh a tree, so that the birds
of the air come and lodge in the branches thereof. (Matthew 13:31–32)

MUSTARD SEED

The variety of mustard plant seen here now grows throughout most of Palestine, its bright yellow blooms blanketing wide fields after the spring rains. Yet we cannot be sure that this particular plant and the mustard plant of which Jesus speaks in the Gospels are one and the same. Jesus speaks of the mustard plant becoming a tree, in the branches of which birds can rest or nest. The modern mustard plant, however, is an annual which in general hardly grows to bush size, although it has been known to reach a height of ten feet by the Sea of Galilee. The bush bears the weight of small birds but is usually not strong enough to support nests. The seeds of the modern plant, like the seeds of the plant of which Jesus speaks, are very small.

Another parable spake he unto them; The kingdom of heaven is like unto leaven, which a woman took, and hid in three measures of meal, till the whole was leavened. (Matthew 13:33)

LEAVEN

In Biblical times the preparation of bread in the home was woman's special assignment. She was the baker, as is true among the Bedouin of today. Her oven was usually hive-shaped or cylindrical in form, made of coarse clay, and occasionally reinforced with brick or stone. Remains of ovens have been found throughout Palestine, and some of these may date back to prehistoric times.

In one form of the oven, thin dough was thrown against the heated inner wall so that both sides of the bread would be baked. In a second and more conventional form, the oven was divided into a lower area for the fire and an upper area with its flat stone surface for baking.

Bread was leavened by using dough that had been reserved from an earlier batch. The woman "hid" or mixed this in the new dough "till the whole was leavened." Three measures of meal were usually sufficient for an average family's daily needs. The Greek word used in the parable shows that the woman was using wheat flour.

Again, the kingdom of heaven is like unto a net, that was cast into the sea, and gathered of every kind: which, when it was full, they drew to shore, and sat down, and gathered the good into vessels, but cast the bad away. (Matthew 13:47–48)

DRAWNET

The use of nets in the Middle East dates back to Mesolithic times. In the time of Jesus two types of net were used on the Sea of Galilee: first, the hand net, made of flax or hemp and weighted on the outer edges, designed to be cast by an individual over a limited area; and second, the larger drawnet or seine, also of hemp or flax. The latter was weighted on one edge but had floats attached to the other edge. Usually handled from a boat, it required more than one person to set it and draw it in. The Greek term which underlies the word for net (found in this passage of the Gospel of Matthew) identifies it as a drawnet.

For all these things do the nations of the world seek after: and your Father knoweth that ye have need of these things. But rather seek ye the kingdom of God; and all these things shall be added unto you. Fear not, little flock; for it is your Father's good pleasure to give you the kingdom. (Luke 12:30–32)

GRAZING SHEEP

The sheep found in Palestine during the Biblical period was the species known as the fat-tailed sheep (*Ovis laticaudata*), so named because its tail developed a thick, heavy mass of fat. These sheep flourished on the marginal pasturage found in the hill country of Judaea, and as a result an economy developed there which counted its wealth in flocks and which was managed by shepherd-kings.

And the Jews' passover was at hand, and Jesus went up to Jerusalem, and found in the temple those that sold oxen and sheep and doves, and the changers of money sitting: and when he had made a scourge of small cords, he drove them all out of the temple, and the sheep, and the oxen; and poured out the changers' money, and overthrew the tables; and said unto them that sold doves, Take these things hence; make not my Father's house an house of merchandise.   (John 2:13–16)

MONEYCHANGING IN THE TEMPLE

Some of "the ones who sat at table" in the outer court of the temple in Jerusalem were marked as moneychangers by the silver half-shekel they wore in the ear. Such persons rendered a service useful to worshipers coming to pay their temple tax or purchase their sacrifice, and for that service the moneychangers exacted a fee, traditionally one twenty-fourth of a shekel. The moneychanger not only changed local coins into various denominations, but also changed foreign coins into local currency. Thus Jews from far and wide could pay the half-shekel temple tax required of them by Scripture (Exodus 30:13–15).

To pious Jews all portraiture was a profanation, a violation of the Old Testament commandment against graven images. Further, some of the emperors looked upon themselves as divine and had themselves or members of their family depicted as gods or goddesses on their coins. The pious Jew, though forced to use the hated Roman coinage in his daily life, would at least be able to exchange Roman coinage for coinage without portraiture or reference to pagan gods. With that "purer" money he would then buy a sacrificial animal.

Shown here is a model of the Temple Mount as seen from the south. Moneychanging probably would have occurred within or near the long colonnaded building, in the background, known as the "Royal Portico."

When therefore the Lord knew how the Pharisees had heard that Jesus made and baptized more disciples than John, (though Jesus himself baptized not, but his disciples,) he left Judaea, and departed again into Galilee. And he must needs go through Samaria. (John 4:1–4)

VALLEY IN SAMARIA

A traveler who walked the ancient road north from Jerusalem, after most of a day's journey, would have been aware of a striking change in the countryside. Behind him lay the high tableland that marked Judaea, and in front of him lay Samaria, whose mountainous terrain was cut by many deep, wide, and fertile valleys. Mount Judah, with its high natural barriers and isolation from surrounding lands and people, stands in sharp contrast to Mount Ephraim, where valleys stretch out east, west, and north, and thereby leave Samaria open to commerce and conquest. Historically, the hill country of Judaea was easily defended and seldom captured, while Samaria, with little natural defense, was regularly overrun by invaders.

Jews regarded the Samaritans as descendants of some of those invaders and their transplanted captives, and therefore looked down upon them as a people of mixed stock. Jews worshiped God in the temple in Jerusalem; they studied the law (*Torah*), the prophets, and the songs of praise, as preserved in the books of the Old Testament. Samaritans, on the other hand, accepted only the first five books of the Old Testament and insisted that God was to be worshiped on Mount Gerizim. Strict observers of the law, the Samaritans regarded Jews as lax and apostate in their worship of God.

For these reasons, Jews often avoided traveling north via Samaria, even though it might be the most direct route. John, in his Gospel, gives us a hint of this when he states that Jesus "must needs go through Samaria." It was into Samaria, then, and among the Samaritans, that Jesus traveled when he descended into the valley seen here.

Then cometh he to a city of Samaria, which is called Sychar, near to the parcel of ground that Jacob gave to his son Joseph. Now Jacob's well was there. Jesus therefore, being wearied with his journey, sat thus on the well: and it was about the sixth hour. There cometh a woman of Samaria to draw water: Jesus saith unto her, Give me to drink. (For his disciples were gone away unto the city to buy meat.) (John 4:5–8)

JACOB'S WELL

The Well of Jacob, renowned for the sweetness of its water, is about two days' travel by foot on the ancient way between Jerusalem and Samaria. The Gospel records that "it was about the sixth hour" when Jesus arrived—that is, about our noon hour.

This is one of the most widely accepted New Testament sites in the Holy Land today. The ancient well is hand-dug, stone-lined, and one of the deepest in Palestine. Today, it lies obscured in the crypt of a nearly completed modern church, the latest of several churches which have been built over the well in the past fifteen hundred years. Arculf, a pilgrim on his way to Jerusalem in A.D. 670, recorded the depth of Jacob's Well as "forty times the span of a man's arms." Modern measurements indicate that the well is now only about half that depth.

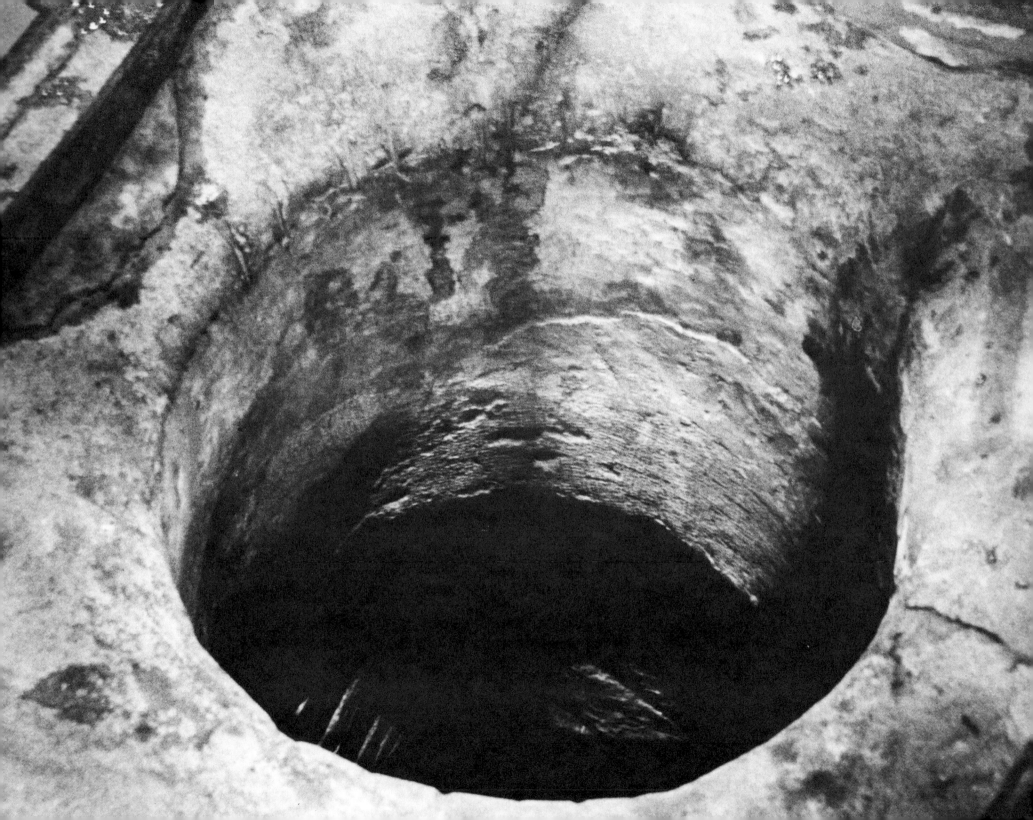

Jesus answered and said unto her, If thou knewest the gift of God, and who it is that saith to thee, Give me to drink; thou wouldest have asked of him, and he would have given thee living water. The woman saith unto him, Sir, thou hast nothing to draw with, and the well is deep: from whence then hast thou that living water? Art thou greater than our father Jacob, which gave us the well, and drank thereof himself, and his children, and his cattle?. . . Our fathers worshipped in this mountain; and ye say, that in Jerusalem is the place where men ought to worship. Jesus saith unto her, Woman, believe me, the hour cometh, when ye shall neither in this mountain, nor yet at Jerusalem, worship the Father. . . But the hour cometh, and now is, when the true worshippers shall worship the Father in spirit and in truth: for the Father seeketh such to worship him. (John 4:10–12, 20–21, 23)

MOUNT GERIZIM

It was on nearby Mount Gerizim that, some 300 years before Jesus lived, the Samaritans had built their temple, similar to the one in Jerusalem where the Jews worshiped. This imposing structure, however, had been destroyed about 150 years before the Gospel conversation between Jesus and the Samaritan woman at Jacob's Well. Only recently have archaeologists uncovered the monumental temple platform, from the top of which one can see the location of the well in the valley below. In fact, by means of a theodolite and a simple trigonometric calculation, it has now been shown that the woman beside the ancient wellhead would have been able to see clearly the ruins of her forefathers' temple.

The ruins of the ancient city of Shechem (Tell Balatah) are near the Well of Jacob. The Old Testament mentions this as the city to which Abraham first came in the land of Canaan and it was here that Jacob is recorded as buying "the parcel of ground" which he "gave to his son Joseph." Shechem later became the chief city of the Samaritans.

Now there is at Jerusalem by the sheep market a pool, which is called in the Hebrew tongue Bethesda, having five porches. In these lay a great multitude of impotent folk, of blind, halt, withered. . . . .And a certain man was there, which had an infirmity thirty and eight years. When Jesus saw him lie, and knew that he had been now a long time in that case, he saith unto him, Wilt thou be made whole? The impotent man answered him, Sir, I have no man, when the water is troubled, to put me into the pool: but while I am coming, another steppeth down before me. Jesus saith unto him, Rise, take up thy bed, and walk. (John 5:2–3, 5–8)

POOL OF BETHESDA

Bethesda, "house of outpouring" or, based upon a slight variant, "house of mercy," was the name of a pool near the passageway in the wall of Jerusalem, north of the temple area, known as the Sheep Gate. The name Bethesda was applied both to the pool and to the district of Jerusalem in which it lay.

The text of the "Copper Scroll," written in the first century A.D. and found in Cave III of the Dead Sea Scroll Caves, indicates that at Bethesda there were to be found not one pool but two, and both the Gospel account and several later sources record that the pool had five porticoes. This last odd number made the shape of Bethesda's pools difficult to envision before their excavation. Lying some 60 feet below modern ground level, near the present St. Stephen's Gate and the nearby Church of St. Ann, the pools, each about 200 feet long and 160 feet wide, were found to lie side by side and were separated by a dike 20 feet thick. Columns, capitals and other architectural members fallen in the pool areas have made possible a tentative reconstruction of the five porticoes. Four of the columned porch-like structures, each about 30 feet high, originally surrounded the double pool, one located on each side. The fifth portico, built upon the dike which separated the two pools, joined the two longer porticoes at their midpoint.

No clear explanation has been given why, on occasion, the waters of the pool became "troubled."

And Herod said, John have I beheaded: but who is this, of whom I hear such things? And he desired to see him. (Luke 9:9)

When Jesus heard of it, he departed (Matthew 14:13) *. . . and went aside privately into a desert place belonging to the city called Bethsaida.* (Luke 9:10) *. . .and when the people had heard thereof, they followed him on foot out of the cities.* (Matthew 14:13)

When Jesus then lifted up his eyes, and saw a great company come unto him, he saith unto Philip, Whence shall we buy bread, that these may eat? (John 6:5)

LOAVES

Bethsaida, "house of the fishermen," the city from which Peter, Andrew, and Philip came, was located, as indicated in the Gospel record, on the shore of the Sea of Galilee. Other literary evidence mentions that Bethsaida, originally a small town, was later rebuilt by Philip the Tetrarch. Greatly enlarged, it was given the rank and title of city during the first decade of the first century A.D. The new city was named Bethsaida Julias in honor of the daughter of the emperor Augustus, Augusta Julia.

Bethsaida Julias has not been excavated. Its remains may lie buried in a mound called et Tell on the east side of the Jordan River about one mile from the northern shore of the Sea of Galilee. An aqueduct and a Roman road run in its direction, all of which indicates that a city of some importance may lie buried there. Another small mound or *tell,* Khirbet et Araj, located south of Bethsaida Julias on the coast of the Sea of Galilee beside the mouth of the Jordan River, has a natural harbor. Marble columns and architectural fragments have been found nearby. It has been suggested that the smaller mound at the edge of the sea was the port or harbor of Bethsaida and the place where fishermen would have landed their boats.

Barley loaves were the common man's meal in Biblical times. They were made with whole-grain flour, baked in the cool of the early morning of the same day they were to be eaten. As such, they would have been tasty and fresh, whereas a day later, without preservation, they would have become hard and unpalatable.

One of his disciples, Andrew, Simon Peter's brother, saith unto him, There is a lad here, which hath five barley loaves, and two small fishes: but what are they among so many?
(John 6:8–9)

And he commanded them to make all sit down by companies upon the green grass. . . . And when he had taken the five loaves and the two fishes, he looked up to heaven, and blessed, and brake the loaves, and gave them to his disciples to set before them; and the two fishes divided he among them all. And they did all eat, and were filled. And they took up twelve baskets full of the fragments, and of the fishes.   (Mark 6:39, 41–43)

And they that had eaten were about five thousand men, beside women and children.
(Matthew 14:21)

FISHES

The fish of this Gospel episode could have been any of many small fish which live in the Sea of Galilee, such as perch, carp, or barbels, among others. They were undoubtedly not the scaleless catfish which, though it lives there, was prohibited by Jewish food laws (Leviticus 11:9–10). Since the fish were ready to be eaten, they probably had already been salt-cured. The industry of fish curing and drying was a well-known one in this area in the first century A.D.

And when even was now come, his disciples went down unto the sea, and entered into a ship, and went over the sea toward Capernaum. And it was now dark, and Jesus was not come to them.   (John 6:16–17)

DARKNESS AT GALILEE

The Sea of Galilee lies below sea level in a geological depression formed by the steep hills of Gilead to the east and the equally steep hills of Galilee to the west. Within the narrow confines of this small valley the days are short. Sunrise comes over the eastern heights late, and twilight settles early as the afternoon sun is obscured by the rim of the western hills. It was in this narrow valley of shortened days and lengthened nights that Jesus spent the greater part of his ministry.

And the sea arose by reason of a great wind that blew. (John 6:18)

And he saw them toiling in rowing; for the wind was contrary unto them: and about the fourth watch of the night he cometh unto them, walking upon the sea. . . . And immediately he talked with them, and saith unto them, Be of good cheer: it is I; be not afraid. And he went up unto them into the ship; and the wind ceased. . . . (Mark 6:48, 50–51)

. . . and immediately the ship was at the land whither they went. (John 6:21)

WALKING UPON THE SEA

The Sea of Galilee, with its compact size, pleasant setting, and usually placid surface, leaves the visitor to its shores unprepared for the violence of the storms which can sweep across it. In winter, hot dry windstorms blow with destructive force from the eastern desert. In summer, cool air borne by westerly winds sweeps down the treeless slopes west of the sea and strikes the hot humid air that accumulates over its surface. This can generate sudden squalls and local storms which churn up the surface of the water to such a degree that small boats may capsize.

And thou, Capernaum, which art exalted unto heaven, shalt be brought down to hell: for if the mighty works, which have been done in thee, had been done in Sodom, it would have remained until this day.   (Matthew 11:23)

SODOM

The exact location of the city of Sodom is not known, though it probably lies at the southern end of the Dead Sea near Jebel Usdum, the Mountain of Sodom, a great mass of salt which rises on the western shore of the sea. It is possible that the remains of the city lie submerged in shallow water about midway between the eastern and western shores. Recent underwater exploration in the area has uncovered some linear configurations on the sea bottom which are thought to show the lines of stone walls, although stones removed from there were so salt-encrusted and disordered as to raise doubts about their origin.

　　While the exact location of Sodom may no longer be known, Josephus (a contemporary of Paul) reported that the ruins were still visible in his day.

And he said also to the people, When ye see a cloud rise out of the west, straightway ye say, There cometh a shower; and so it is. And when ye see the south wind blow, ye say, There will be heat; and it cometh to pass. (Luke 12:54–55)

. . . When it is evening, ye say, It will be fair weather: for the sky is red. And in the morning, It will be foul weather to day: for the sky is red and lowring. O ye hypocrites, ye can discern the face of the sky; but can ye not discern the signs of the times? (Matthew 16:2–3)

SIGNS OF THE TIMES

Because of the naturally mild climate, the people of Palestine have for countless generations spent most of their lives out-of-doors. In Bible times they worked, ate, and slept outside. Shepherds watched over their flocks by night, farmers guarded their harvest, fishermen fished the night through. People saw sunrise and sunset, observed the progression of the seasons, knew the locations of the stars and the movement of the planets.

So often unconfined by wall or roof, people would have early learned to recognize those signs which foretold the change of weather. They knew that the prevailing westerly winds brought dark clouds filled with rain; that the scorching south wind from the desert brought dry air laden with dust, which parched the skin and hurt the eyes. If the sun set red, it augured fair weather; if the sun rose amid red clouds, a storm was sure to follow.

And from thence he arose, and went into the borders of Tyre and Sidon, and entered into an house, and would have no man know it: but he could not be hid. . . . And again, departing from the coasts of Tyre and Sidon, he came unto the sea of Galilee, through the midst of the coasts of Decapolis. And they bring unto him one that was deaf, and had an impediment in his speech; and they beseech him to put his hand upon him. . . . And straightway his ears were opened, and the string of his tongue was loosed, and he spake plain. (Mark 7:24, 31–32, 35)

A DECAPOLIS CITY

The successors of Alexander the Great, including veterans of his army, established cities and colonies in the Middle East which became centers of Greek trade, culture, and language. By the New Testament period, a loose confederation of these Greek cities, calling themselves Decapolis, or "Ten Cities," had been established to the east of the Jordan River and the Sea of Galilee. The list of cities varies, but usually includes Scythopolis (Beth-shean), Hippos, Gadara, Pella, Philadelphia (Ammon), Gerasa, Dion, Canatha, Damascus, and Raphana. Of these, Scythopolis is the only city which lay west of the Jordan. Few of these cities have been excavated, but the location of most of them is known, so that the area of Jesus' travels can be generally defined.

One of the most evident of the cities is Hippos (Sussita or Qal 'at el-Husn). The acropolis of that city (atop the conical hill in the photograph) is close by the eastern shore of the Sea of Galilee, almost directly east of Tiberias. Although Hippos has not been excavated, there are enough surface remains to indicate that Jesus and his disciples would have seen there a planned city with colonnaded streets, a theater, an aqueduct, and a fortified high place, much like other Greek cities of the day.

And Jesus went out, and his disciples, into the towns of Caesarea Philippi: and by the way he asked his disciples, saying unto them, Whom do men say that I am? And they answered, John the Baptist: but some say, Elias; and others, One of the prophets. And he saith unto them, But whom say ye that I am? And Peter answereth and saith unto him, Thou art the Christ.
(Mark 8:27–29)

And Jesus answered and said unto him, Blessed art thou, Simon Bar-jona: for flesh and blood hath not revealed it unto thee, but my Father which is in heaven. And I say also unto thee, That thou art Peter, and upon this rock I will build my church; and the gates of hell shall not prevail against it. . . . Then charged he his disciples that they should tell no man that he was Jesus the Christ.   (Matthew 16:17–18, 20)

CAESAREA PHILIPPI

Of the thirteen towns and cities in the Roman Empire each named Caesarea, two were located in Palestine. One of these was built by Herod on the coast of the Mediterranean and called Caesarea Maritima. The other, located in the northern part of Palestine where one source of the Jordan River flows out of a cave, was an ancient city called Paneas. Renamed Caesarea by Philip the Tetrarch in the first century A.D., it came to be known as Caesarea Philippi.

In the period of the Old Testament the god Baal was probably worshiped at this water source. With the coming of the Greeks, the worship of Baal gave way to the worship of Pan, the god of forest, flock, and shepherd. As a result of this change, the city and district became known as Paneas, the remembrance of which is retained in its modern Arabic name of Baniyas.

When Jesus asked his disciples to tell him who they thought he was, the question was posed against a backdrop which included the tumbling water source of the Jordan, the groves in the rock where Pan was revered, and the white marble temple which King Herod had erected to the Roman emperor Augustus Caesar.

And, behold, there talked with him two men, which were Moses and Elias: who appeared in glory, and spake of his decease which he should accomplish at Jerusalem. (Luke 9:30–31)

. . . a bright cloud overshadowed them. . . . (Matthew 17:5)

And there came a voice out of the cloud, saying, This is my beloved Son: hear him. And when the voice was past, Jesus was found alone. And they kept it close, and told no man in those days any of those things which they had seen. (Luke 9:35–36)

A BRIGHT CLOUD

The Gospel account says only that Jesus took his disciples "up into an high mountain" and it was there that the Transfiguration took place. The mountain's location is obscure, some scholars favoring Mount Tabor (seen here), others the more distant (and usually snow-clad) Mount Hermon. By the sixth century, three churches had been built on Mount Tabor in memory of the three tabernacles which Peter proposed at the time of the Transfiguration.

And when they were come to the multitude, there came to him a certain man, kneeling down to him, and saying, Lord, have mercy on my son: for he is lunatick, and sore vexed. . . . (Matthew 17:14–15)

Jesus said unto him, If thou canst believe, all things are possible to him that believeth. And straightway the father of the child cried out, and said with tears, Lord, I believe; help thou mine unbelief. (Mark 9:23–24)

And Jesus rebuked the devil; and he departed out of him: and the child was cured from that very hour. Then came the disciples to Jesus apart, and said, Why could not we cast him out? And Jesus said unto them, Because of your unbelief: for verily I say unto you, If ye have faith as a grain of mustard seed, ye shall say unto this mountain, Remove hence to yonder place; and it shall remove; and nothing shall be impossible unto you. (Matthew 17:18–20)

REMOVING A MOUNTAIN

After spring rain, or when there is reduced haze in the Jordan Valley, one becomes aware of the ghostly white eminence of Mount Hermon looming on the distant horizon to the north. At such times its snowcapped peak can be seen reflected on the surface of the Sea of Galilee.

Mount Hermon is by far the tallest mountain in or near Palestine, rising to a height of 9,100 feet above sea level and extending in length over twenty miles. Snow lies on its summit throughout the year, though it diminishes considerably during the hot dry summers.

In the foreground of the photograph are mustard plants in bloom, some nearly six feet in height. It is a scene probably quite similar to that viewed by Jesus and his disciples during the events described in the Gospels.

And it came to pass, that, as they went in the way, a certain man said unto him, Lord, I will follow thee whithersoever thou goest. . . . And another also said, Lord, I will follow thee; but let me first go bid them farewell, which are at home at my house. And Jesus said unto him, No man, having put his hand to the plough, and looking back, is fit for the kingdom of God. (Luke 9:57, 61–62)

PLOW

The plowpoints used throughout Palestine in the Biblical period were neither meant for nor capable of turning a furrow, but were simply iron spikes designed to be dragged through the topsoil of the land, penetrating little deeper than the span of a man's hand.

Without moist subsoil turned over in furrows to contrast with the unplowed portion of the field, the plowman would have had to be all the more diligent to plow parallel to the previous and barely discernible scratch lines. He also had to be ever alert for stones, which were practically everywhere. To look back while plowing in such soil, amid such stones and with such equipment, was to risk a missed plowline or to shatter a plowpoint on a stone or bedrock.

And Jesus answering said, A certain man went down from Jerusalem to Jericho, and fell among thieves, which stripped him of his raiment, and wounded him, and departed, leaving him half dead. And by chance there came down a certain priest that way: and when he saw him, he passed by on the other side. And likewise a Levite, when he was at the place, came and looked on him, and passed by on the other side. But a certain Samaritan, as he journeyed, came where he was: and when he saw him, he had compassion on him, and went to him, and bound up his wounds, pouring in oil and wine, and set him on his own beast, and brought him to an inn, and took care of him. . . . Which now of these three, thinkest thou, was neighbour unto him that fell among the thieves? . . . Go, and do thou likewise.
(Luke 10:30–34, 36, 37)

GOOD SAMARITAN

A traveler setting out from Jerusalem to Jericho would be vividly aware of how the land drops away before him and that the controlling direction is *down.* High on the central mountain ridge of the country, 2,500 feet above sea level, Jerusalem is some half-mile higher than, and some twenty miles west of, Jericho, which is located 770 feet below sea level in the Jordan Valley. Because of the steepness of the decline, the road turns tortuously in switchback after switchback, thereby reducing the rate of descent and making it possible for man and beast to travel the road with greater ease.

Whether the traveler was ascending or descending, the pace would have been slow. A modern hiker, retracing the road as it was in Roman times, required six hours to walk down to Jericho and nearly eight hours to walk up to Jerusalem. The road crosses part of the Wilderness of Judaea, an area almost devoid of life where, in Bible times, hills and gullies afforded ample place for highwaymen to hide and prey upon travelers.

Early rabbinical evidence points to an inn that provided care for travelers on the Jerusalem-Jericho road. A late tradition locates it about twelve miles east of Jerusalem at a pass which cuts through the red marl deposits seen here, called by local inhabitants Tal 'at ed-Damm, ''the ascent of blood.''

And when they were come to Capernaum, they that received tribute money came to Peter, and said, Doth not your master pay tribute? He saith, Yes. And when he was come into the house, Jesus prevented him, saying, What thinkest thou, Simon? of whom do the kings of the earth take custom or tribute? of their own children, or of strangers? Peter saith unto him, Of strangers. Jesus saith unto him, Then are the children free. Notwithstanding, lest we should offend them, go thou to the sea, and cast an hook, and take up the fish that first cometh up; and when thou hast opened his mouth, thou shalt find a piece of money: that take, and give unto them for me and thee. (Matthew 17:24–27)

THE TRIBUTE MONEY

One of the more abundant types of fish caught in the Sea of Galilee is *Tilapia galilala*, known locally as Saint Peter's fish. Perhaps because it is so plentiful and is such excellent food, it became the best known of the fish caught in the Sea of Galilee and thereby was assumed to have been the fish which Peter caught.

How think ye? if a man have an hundred sheep, and one of them be gone astray, doth he not leave the ninety and nine, and goeth into the mountains, and seeketh that which is gone astray?. . . .Even so it is not the will of your Father which is in heaven, that one of these little ones should perish. (Matthew 18:12, 14)

THE SHEEP THAT STRAYED

The figure of a shepherd carrying over his shoulder a wounded, lost, or lame sheep was, and is, a common sight wherever in the Holy Land flocks are kept. Straying sheep which lose their way or sustain injury are extremely vulnerable and must be quickly found and carried or led back to the fold.

In the Christian community, the figure of the Good Shepherd bearing a sheep over his shoulders was one of the earliest and most widespread representations of Christ. It could be seen across the whole of the Roman Empire from Britain to Dura Europos on the Euphrates, depicted in stone, fresco, and mosaic.

And as Jesus passed by, he saw a man which was blind from his birth. And his disciples asked him, saying, Master, who did sin, this man, or his parents, that he was born blind? Jesus answered, Neither hath this man sinned, nor his parents: but that the works of God should be made manifest in him. . . . When he had thus spoken, he spat on the ground, and made clay of the spittle, and he anointed the eyes of the blind man with the clay, and said unto him, Go, wash in the pool of Siloam, (which is by interpretation, Sent). He went his way therefore, and washed, and came seeing. (John 9:1–3, 6–7)

POOL OF SILOAM

The Pool of Siloam is mentioned twice in the New Testament and appears in the Old Testament as the pool of Siloah (Nehemiah 3:15) and Shiloah (Isaiah 8:6). It is identified with present-day Birket Silwan, a pool in Jerusalem, which receives its water through the 1,750-foot tunnel from Gihon Spring constructed during the reign of Judaean King Hezekiah (see II Kings 20:20; II Chronicles 32:30).

A Hebrew inscription was discovered nearly a century ago just inside the tunnel from the present pool. The message, carved in stone, details the meeting deep under Jerusalem, of the two ancient drilling teams which cut the lengthy aqueduct in the eighth century B.C. The presence of such an ancient inscription may have been unknown even to Jesus' contemporaries.

A fifth-century A.D. church was built over the Pool of Siloam site to commemorate the healing of the blind man. Little remains of the church and the porticoes which were said to have been built there. They probably lie buried under a small mosque, the minaret of which marks the location of Birket Silwan, where Arab women still come to wash their clothes.

. . . after that he saith unto them, Our friend Lazarus sleepeth; but I go, that I may awake him out of sleep. Then said his disciples, Lord, if he sleep, he shall do well. . . . Then said Jesus unto them plainly, Lazarus is dead. . . . Then when Jesus came, he found that he had lain in the grave four days already. . . . It was a cave, and a stone lay upon it. Jesus said, Take ye away the stone. . . . And Jesus lifted up his eyes, and said, Father, I thank thee that thou hast heard me. And I knew that thou hearest me always. . . . And when he thus had spoken, he cried with a loud voice, Lazarus, come forth. And he that was dead came forth, bound hand and foot with graveclothes: and his face was bound about with a napkin. Jesus saith unto them, Loose him, and let him go. (John 11:11–12, 14, 17, 38–39, 41–44)

LAZARUS' TOMB

On the southeastern slopes of the Mount of Olives is the town of Bethany, where, since the fourth century, pilgrims have been shown the ''Tomb of Lazarus.'' A modern church complex nearby has elements of earlier churches dating back to the fifth century. The tomb itself may be approached by a long vaulted and stepped passage which leads to a vestibule, through the floor of which a partly hewn burial cave may be entered. Within the burial chamber, which is about eight feet square, are three raised stone shelves, each hewn from the sides of the chamber and each designed to receive a single body. The entrance to the burial chamber, it is assumed, would have been covered by laying a flat stone across the opening in the floor of the vestibule. Other tombs of this type from the Roman period have been discovered in the vicinity of Jerusalem. In fact, in one instance, ossuaries found in a first-century tomb located close to Bethany bear three familiar names: Lazarus, Martha, and Mary.

One indication that Bethany has long been thought of as the site of the tomb of Lazarus is to be found in the Arabic name for Bethany, el-'Azariyeh, a term which preserves Lazarus' name.

Then Jesus six days before the passover came to Bethany, where Lazarus was which had been dead, whom he raised from the dead. . . .Much people of the Jews therefore knew that he was there: and they came not for Jesus' sake only, but that they might see Lazarus also, whom he had raised from the dead. (John 12:1, 9)

And when they drew nigh unto Jerusalem, and were come to Bethphage, unto the mount of Olives, then sent Jesus two disciples, saying unto them, Go into the village over against you, and straightway ye shall find an ass tied, and a colt with her: loose them, and bring them unto me. . . . All this was done, that it might be fulfilled which was spoken by the prophet, saying, Tell ye the daughter of Sion, Behold, thy King cometh unto thee, meek, and sitting upon an ass, and a colt the foal of an ass. (Matthew 21:1–2, 4–5, quoting Zechariah 9:9)

. . . and they set Jesus thereon. (Luke 19:35)

And the multitudes that went before, and that followed, cried, saying, Hosanna to the Son of David. . . . (Matthew 21:9)

. . . Blessed is the King of Israel that cometh in the name of the Lord. . . . These things understood not his disciples at the first: but when Jesus was glorified, then remembered they that these things were written of him. . . . (John 12:13, 16)

BETHPHAGE

Although Bethphage's exact location is uncertain, we know of the town from the Gospel account as well as from rabbinical literature. In the Talmud, Bethphage is described as part of the suburbs of Jerusalem, probably at its easternmost limit. Bethphage can be regarded, then, as the start of Jesus' triumphal entry into Jerusalem.

When Jesus, who had walked the length and breadth of Palestine and, to the best of our knowledge, had never ridden, elected to ride a donkey the short distance into Jerusalem from Bethphage, the significance of his act would not have been missed by those who watched his journey. Nearly one thousand years before, not far from this same spot, Solomon, "Son of David" and newly-anointed King of Israel, had entered Jerusalem on the back of a mule, accompanied by the hosannas of the people.

And when he was come near, he beheld the city, and wept over it. (Luke 19:41)

And when he was come into Jerusalem, all the city was moved, saying, Who is this?
(Matthew 21:10)

THE GOLDEN GATE

The "Golden Gate," also called the Gate of Mercy or Eastern Gate, was built in the seventh century A.D.
and is located in the eastern wall of the city of Jerusalem. It was the only gate on that side of the city which
gave direct access to the temple area. A late tradition says that the present gate is built at the place where
Jesus made his triumphal entry into Jerusalem. There is some archaeological evidence of an earlier gate
where the present gate stands as well as some indication of a roadway that earlier crossed over the
Kidron Valley at that point. An early Jewish tradition said that it would be through this gate that the Messiah
would come, and, as a result, many people arranged to be buried near the gate to be ready for that event.

Fearful that the Messiah might come again through the Golden Gate of Jerusalem and thus deprive
him of the city, the Turkish governor of Jerusalem in A.D. 1530 ordered the sealing of the gate to prevent any
passage whatever.

And they send unto him certain of the Pharisees and of the Herodians, to catch him in his words. (Mark 12:13)

. . . so they might deliver him unto the power and authority of the governor. And they asked him, saying, Master, we know that thou sayest and teachest rightly. . . . Is it lawful for us to give tribute unto Caesar, or no? (Luke 20:20–22)

Shall we give, or shall we not give? (Mark 12:15)

But he perceived their craftiness, and said unto them, Why tempt ye me? (Luke 20:23)

Shew me the tribute money. And they brought unto him a penny. (Matthew 22:19)

Whose image and superscription hath it? They answered and said, Caesar's. And he said unto them, Render therefore unto Caesar the things which be Caesar's, and unto God the things which be God's. (Luke 20:24–25)

RENDER UNTO CAESAR

The Greek word translated above as "penny" is *dēnarion,* and the coin in question was probably the silver denarius of Tiberius, the current Caesar. Of the three types of denarii issued during this emperor's reign, the one shown here was by far the most common. The coin's obverse has the head of Tiberius depicted on it, as well as a legend which reads TIBERIUS CAESAR DIVI AUGUSTI FILIUS AUGUSTUS, that is, "Emperor Tiberius Caesar son of the divine Augustus." The reverse of the coin shows the Emperor's mother, Livia Drusilla, enthroned as the earthly incarnation of Pax, "peace." PONTIFEX MAXIMUS completes the legend begun on the obverse and identifies Tiberius as the "chief priest" of the Imperial Cult. This coin, called the "tribute penny," was used by the people of Palestine to pay their tax to Rome and was, in turn, the money used to pay the troops who occupied the land. (Photograph courtesy of the Israel Museum, Jerusalem)

And Jesus sat over against the treasury. . . .   (Mark 12:41)

And he looked up, and saw the rich men casting their gifts into the treasury. And he saw also a certain poor widow casting in thither two mites. And he said, Of a truth I say unto you, that this poor widow hath cast in more than they all. . .   (Luke 21:1–3)

For all they did cast in of their abundance; but she of her want did cast in all that she had, even all her living.   (Mark 12:44)

WIDOW'S MITES

The coin which, in the King James Version, is called a "mite" is referred to in the Greek text as a *lepton,* whose value was half that of a *quadrans.* The lepton was the smallest Greek copper coin and the quadrans the smallest Roman. The Roman government strictly controlled the issuance of money but allowed local mints, under supervision, to issue coins in copper. Because the Jews were affronted by portraiture of any kind, some local coinage minted in Palestine bore no portraits.

Pictured here is a lepton issued by a local mint in Palestine during the reign of the emperor Tiberius. This coin and similar ones issued under the Procurators would have been referred to generally in Greek as leptons or in Latin as a half quadrans. The legend on the obverse (at left) indicates that the coin was issued in the reign of Tiberius Caesar. In the center is the crook or *lituus,* the staff of the priest of the Imperial Cult, of which Tiberius was chief priest. The reverse of the coin (at right) shows a wreath with berries and the letters LIH, denoting that the coin was issued in the eighteenth year of the reign of Tiberius or, in modern terms, A.D. 31/32.   (Photograph courtesy of the Israel Museum, Jerusalem)

Woe unto you, scribes and Pharisees, hypocrites! for ye are like unto whited sepulchres, which indeed appear beautiful outward, but are within full of dead men's bones, and of all uncleanness. Even so ye also outwardly appear righteous unto men, but within ye are full of hypocrisy and iniquity. (Matthew 23:27, 28)

WHITED SEPULCHRES

Four tombs, all with Hellenistic or Roman architectural style, line the eastern slope of the Kidron Valley. They were probably there in Jesus' day and are today the most evident and imposing tombs to be seen from the neighboring walls of Jerusalem. The "Tomb of Absalom" (seen at the far left) is, properly speaking, not a tomb but a tomb monument. Its lower part is a square monolith cut from the limestone cliff and adorned on its four sides with Ionic columns, a Doric frieze, and an Egyptian cornice. Above the square base is a cylindrical stone pedestal on top of which is a concave conical roof which rises to a height of over fifty feet. In II Samuel 18:18, Absalom is recorded as having set up a "pillar" in his own honor in the Valley of the King (Kidron Valley). Its location is not known and was probably not known in Jesus' day either. In the course of time, the tomb monument became associated with the "pillar of Absalom" and later was simply called the "Tomb of Absalom." The "Tomb of Jehoshaphat" (barely visible in the photograph) lies directly behind the monument.

To the south of the "Tomb of Absalom" is a rock-cut portico with two columns and two pilasters in the Doric order, called the "Tomb of James." A Hebrew inscription on the architrave properly identifies the structure as the tomb of the sons of Hezir, a family of priests from Jerusalem. The name of James, brother of Jesus and early leader of the Christian community in Jerusalem, became associated with the tomb because the record of his martyrdom indicates he had been thrown from the "pinnacle of the temple" (the southeast corner of the Temple Mount) which is near this site. The "Tomb of Zechariah" (in the recess at right) is also a sepulchral monument; no tomb has been found in it or related to it. The columns and pilasters carved on the four sides are Ionic and the whole monument is capped by a pyramid.

O Jerusalem, Jerusalem, thou that killest the prophets, and stonest them which are sent unto thee, how often would I have gathered thy children together, even as a hen gathereth her chickens under her wings, and ye would not! (Matthew 23:37)

JERUSALEM

The Jerusalem Jesus turned to, looked upon and wept over was not dissimilar to the Jerusalem viewed from the Mount of Olives today. It was, and is, the Golden City set upon an hill within whose walls and gates is one of the world's prime centers for those who seek peace and worship the one God. It is the same city beside whose walls many who have sought to implement that peace and glorify that God have been stoned, crucified and put to the sword.

And as he went out of the temple, one of his disciples saith unto him, Master, see what manner of stones and what buildings are here!   (Mark 13:1)

And as some spake of the temple, how it was adorned with goodly stones and gifts, he said . . . .   (Luke 21:5)

. . . Seest thou these great buildings? . . . .   (Mark 13:2)

GOODLY STONES

The large limestone blocks which form the support walls around Herod's Temple Mount had their exposed surfaces smoothed flat with fine comb chisels. Cut into the four limits of the face of the stone was a wide depressed border. The dressed blocks were then laid in courses without mortar, each course of stones set back slightly from the course beneath it. In this manner, from foundation trenches carved in the bedrock of the Temple Mount, the walls rose, in some places as high as 36 courses. Josephus tells us that "Some of the stones in the building were 45 cubits in length, 5 in height and 6 in breadth." (*Wars* V, v, 6)

. . . There shall not be left here one stone upon another, that shall not be thrown down.
(Matthew 24:2)

For the days shall come upon thee, that thine enemies shall cast a trench about thee, and compass thee round, and keep thee in on every side, and shall lay thee even with the ground. . . .
(Luke 19:43–44)

And when ye shall see Jerusalem compassed with armies, then know that the desolation thereof is nigh. . . that all things which are written may be fulfilled.   (Luke 21:20, 22)

FALLEN STONES

Clear evidence of Roman destruction of the Temple Mount area has recently been found outside the southern end of the Western Wall. Layer after layer of destruction and occupation debris were removed until the excavators came upon a heavily paved street that ran parallel to the Temple Mount's Western Wall. Clogging this street, and crushing its surface, were hundreds of very large drafted stones. Because of the chisel work on their surface and the type of drafting found around the edges of their face, these stones were judged to have been dislodged from the upper courses of the Herodian wall. Still being built in the time of Jesus, the Herodian Temple complex, after the Jewish Revolt in the first half of the second century A.D., would lay destroyed.

Josephus and Eusebius tell of the trench dug around Jerusalem during the siege by the Roman legions under Titus. Thousands of Jerusalem residents perished from starvation before the capture and destruction of the city about A.D. 70.

Then came the day of unleavened bread, when the passover must be killed. (Luke 22:7)

THE PASSOVER LAMB

The Feast of Passover was celebrated to commemorate the deliverance of Israel from Egypt. It was a solemn feast, in the spring of the year, involving the slaughter of the lamb at the temple, the sprinkling of its blood on the altar, and the eating of its flesh in a ritualized domestic meal by a group of ten or more participants.

Symbolically, the lamb was early associated with Jesus by the primitive Church. It was not lost on his followers that Jesus' crucifixion had occurred during the Passover season.

[Jesus] went forth with his disciples over the brook Cedron. . . . (John 18:1)

And they came to a place which was named Gethsemane. . . . (Mark 14:32)

And Judas also, which betrayed him, knew the place: for Jesus ofttimes resorted thither with his disciples. (John 18:2)

. . . he saith to his disciples, Sit ye here, while I shall pray. (Mark 14:32)

GETHSEMANE

Separating the city of Jerusalem from the Mount of Olives, the Valley of Kidron forms part of the city's natural defenses. In the midst of its narrow valley floor, a brook runs after the winter rains. The Garden of Gethsemane lies across the valley from the Golden Gate on the western slopes of the Mount of Olives and in the Biblical period was probably a garden in the sense that it contained a grove or groves of olive trees. The gardens known today as the Franciscan, the Armenian, and the Russian Gardens are all thought to represent portions of the original Garden of Gethsemane.

And he taketh with him Peter and James and John, and began to be sore amazed, and to be very heavy; and saith unto them, My soul is exceeding sorrowful unto death: tarry ye here, and watch. (Mark 14:33–34)

And he was withdrawn from them about a stone's cast, and kneeled down, and prayed, saying, Father, if thou be willing, remove this cup from me: nevertheless not my will, but thine, be done. (Luke 22:41–42)

AN OLIVE TRUNK

The olive tree grows slowly. In dry places, without irrigation, it may take half a century to reach full production of its fruit. There are trees growing in the western Mediterranean area which are thought to be a thousand years old. The oldest olive trees on the Mount of Olives have been estimated to be between five hundred and seven hundred years of age. Perhaps it was near an ancestor of this gnarled olive tree that Jesus took his three closest disciples and asked them to tarry and to watch.

And being in an agony he prayed more earnestly: and his sweat was as it were great drops of blood falling down to the ground. And when he rose up from prayer, and was come to his disciples, he found them sleeping for sorrow, and said unto them, Why sleep ye? rise and pray, lest ye enter into temptation.   (Luke 22:44–46)

Judas then, having received a band of men and officers from the chief priests and Pharisees, cometh thither with lanterns and torches and weapons.   (John 18:3)

And forthwith he came to Jesus, and said, Hail, master; and kissed him. And Jesus said unto him, Friend, wherefore art thou come?   (Matthew 26:49–50)

. . . betrayest thou the Son of man with a kiss?   (Luke 22:48)

AN OLIVE PRESS

The name "Gethsemane," while not completely understood, may mean "valley of olive oil" or "place of the oil press." Olive oil was highly prized for its value in providing nourishment and light and for its many other uses. It was the ointment of kings. In the press seen here, olives were placed on the circular base and squeezed under the rotating stone, which was originally equipped with a wooden shaft drawn by men or draft animals.

Then Pilate entered into the judgment hall again, and called Jesus, and said unto him, Art thou the King of the Jews? . . . Jesus answered, Thou sayest that I am a king. To this end was I born, and for this cause came I into the world, that I should bear witness unto the truth. . . . Pilate saith unto him, What is truth?   (John 18:33, 37, 38)

And the soldiers led him away into the hall, called Praetorium; and they call together the whole band.   (Mark 15:16)

And the soliders platted a crown of thorns, and put it on his head, and they put on him a purple robe, and said, Hail, King of the Jews! . . . And Pilate saith unto them, Behold the man!
(John 19:2–3, 5)

CROWN OF THORNS

Two types of thornbush grow between the Jordan River and the Mediterranean Sea. The larger bush of the two, *Paliurus spina-christi,* grows to a height of ten feet and is found throughout Israel and western Jordan. It develops long, sharp, recurved thorns which cause the skin to fester when stuck by them. The second thornbush is the *Zizyphus spina-christi.* This is a low scrub whose area of growth is limited to the Jordan Valley, where it is frequently used by Bedouin as a fence to keep goats and cattle out of temporary fields. The scrub thorn seen here would have been less difficult to bend and shape, although the larger bush would have been more readily accessible around Jerusalem.

When he was set down on the judgment seat, his wife sent unto him, saying, Have thou nothing to do with that just man: for I have suffered many things this day in a dream because of him. (Matthew 27:19)

And from thenceforth Pilate sought to release him: but the Jews cried out, saying, If thou let this man go, thou art not Caesar's friend. . . . When Pilate therefore heard that saying, he brought Jesus forth, and sat down in the judgment seat in a place that is called the Pavement, but in the Hebrew, Gabbatha. . . . Then delivered he him therefore unto them to be crucified. And they took Jesus, and led him away. (John 19:12, 13, 16)

GABBATHA

Gabbatha is a term which appears only once in the Bible, and its precise meaning is uncertain. It may mean "open space," and John's Gospel uses it specifically to refer to the paved courtyard where the Roman governor held court. It probably was located beside the Tower of Antonia, a palatial fortification which had been rebuilt by Herod both as his residence and as barracks for soldiers. The tower was referred to by a late Christian source as the Tower of Pilate.

Under the present-day Convent of Our Lady of Zion, an extensive area of large limestone blocks, well worn from traffic, has been uncovered. Some of the stones have scratched upon them games which Roman soldiers and others played while waiting in the courtyard. The stones seen here may be where Jesus stood while on trial before the Roman prefect, Pontius Pilate.

*And he bearing his cross went forth into a place called the place of a skull, which is called in
the Hebrew Golgotha: where they crucified him, and two other with him, on either side one, and
Jesus in the midst. And Pilate wrote a title, and put it on the cross. And the writing was,
JESUS OF NAZARETH THE KING OF THE JEWS. . . . for the place where Jesus was crucified was
nigh to the city: and it was written in Hebrew, and Greek, and Latin. . . . After this, Jesus knowing
that all things were now accomplished, that the scripture might be fulfilled, saith, I thirst. . . .
and they filled a spunge with vinegar, and put it upon hyssop, and put it to his mouth. When
Jesus therefore had received the vinegar, he said, It is finished. . . .* (John 19:17–20, 28–30)

GOLGOTHA

Many visitors to Jerusalem, notably General Gordon of Khartoum, have thought that they could discern
in the craggy side of a low rocky hill, just north of the northern wall of Jerusalem, the shape of a great skull.
(The photograph shows what may be viewed as its two gaping eyes.) The hill became known as Gordon's
Calvary or Skull Hill, and it was thought by some to be Golgotha. While the hill is clearly outside the walls of the
city and may bear some resemblance to Calvary, there is no evidence that this is, in fact, Golgotha.

Though the original site of the Crucifixion is not known with certainty, the traditional site is in what
is now called the Church of the Holy Sepulchre. This is the last of several churches which have stood on the
spot, the first having been erected by Emperor Constantine in A.D. 335 on top of a destroyed shrine, built
earlier by Emperor Hadrian, dedicated to the goddess Venus.

Now in the place where he was crucified there was a garden; and in the garden a new sepulchre, wherein was never man yet laid. (John 19:41)

. . . there came a rich man of Arimathaea, named Joseph, who also himself was Jesus' disciple. . . . And when Joseph had taken the body, he wrapped it in a clean linen cloth. . . . (Matthew 27:57, 59)

There laid they Jesus therefore because of the Jews' preparation day; for the sepulchre was nigh at hand. (John 19:42)

A GARDEN TOMB

The Garden Tomb seen here was discovered accidentally in the nineteenth century close-by Skull Hill or Gordon's Calvary. Although the proximity of the two locations gave impulse to the thesis that here could be found the sites of the Crucifixion and the Resurrection, recent archaeologists have found no solid evidence to support this belief.

The interior of this early tomb consists of two compartments, one designed for family burial, and the other for mourning at the time of interment.

And when the sabbath was past, Mary Magdalene, and Mary the mother of James, and Salome, had bought sweet spices, that they might come and anoint him. And very early in the morning the first day of the week, they came unto the sepulchre at the rising of the sun. And they said among themselves, Who shall roll us away the stone from the door of the sepulchre? And when they looked, they saw that the stone was rolled away: for it was very great.
(Mark 16:1–4)

A ROLLING STONE

Seen here is an ancient tomb with the rolling stone used to seal its entrance. The massive circular hewn stone is five feet in diameter. It stands upright in a slot or track in such fashion as to permit the stone to be rolled across the mouth of the tomb, sealing it, or rolled to one side, as shown, to expose the entrance. A classic example of its type, this tomb of the ''family of Herod'' is located west of the old walled city of Jerusalem and is mentioned by the historian Josephus. Herod's family tomb dates from the first century and would therefore have been contemporary with, and probably similar to, the borrowed tomb where Jesus' body was laid. That tomb, belonging to Joseph of Arimathaea, is described in Matthew 27:57–60 as being new, hewn from rock, and provided with a stone that rolled in front of its entrance—a type that suggests a wealthy owner.

And they entered in, and found not the body of the Lord Jesus. (Luke 24:3)

But Mary stood without at the sepulchre weeping: and as she wept, she stooped down, and looked into the sepulchre, and seeth two angels in white sitting, the one at the head, and the other at the feet, where the body of Jesus had lain. And they say unto her, Woman, why weepest thou? . . . . (John 20:11–13)

. . . Ye seek Jesus of Nazareth, which was crucified: he is risen; he is not here. . . . (Mark 16:6)

. . . Why seek ye the living among the dead? (Luke 24:5)

. . . she turned herself back, and saw Jesus standing, and knew not that it was Jesus. . . . Jesus saith unto her, Mary. She turned herself, and saith unto him, Rabboni; which is to say, Master. (John 20:14, 16)

RESURRECTION

136

And, behold, two of them went that same day to a village called Emmaus, which was from Jerusalem about threescore furlongs. . . . And it came to pass, that, while they communed together and reasoned, Jesus himself drew near, and went with them. But their eyes were holden that they should not know him. . . Then he said unto them, O fools, and slow of heart to believe all that the prophets have spoken: Ought not Christ to have suffered these things, and to enter into his glory? And beginning at Moses and all the prophets, he expounded unto them in all the scriptures the things concerning himself. . . . And their eyes were opened, and they knew him; and he vanished out of their sight. And they said one to another, Did not our heart burn within us, while he talked with us by the way, and while he opened to us the scriptures?   (Luke 24:13, 15–16, 25–27, 31–32)*

WALK TO EMMAUS

Anyone wishing to visit Emmaus meets with the dilemma that there are at least two villages of that name with competing traditions. Part of the problem is that two of our earliest texts of Luke's Gospel give different distances between Jerusalem and Emmaus. One indicates the equivalent of seven miles, while the other gives a figure almost three times that distance. At both distances from Jerusalem, on two different Roman roads, can be found villages which could, in the past, have been designated Emmaus. The town of el Kubeiba lies seven miles northwest of Jerusalem on a secondary Roman road (seen here) which leads from Jerusalem to Diopolis and the Mediterranean coast. Excavations at el Kubeiba have uncovered the remains of a village of the first century and a large Byzantine church of the fifth century A.D. If the disciples left from el Kubeiba, they would have had little trouble retracing their steps to Jerusalem after the evening meal. Josephus and a number of early Christian writers, however, refer to an Emmaus (the town of Amwas today) eighteen miles west of Jerusalem on the Roman highway to Joppa and the seacoast. The similarity of the modern name Amwas to Emmaus supports this possibility. At Amwas have been uncovered structures of the fourth and fifth centuries as well as a large Christian basilica of the sixth century. From Amwas, it would have been difficult (though not impossible) for the disciples, with the day "far spent," to walk eighteen miles up the steep road to Jerusalem.

After these things Jesus shewed himself again to the disciples at the sea of Tiberias. . .
when the morning was now come, Jesus stood on the shore: but the disciples knew not that it
was Jesus. Then Jesus saith unto them, Children, have ye any meat? They answered him,
No. And he said unto them, Cast the net on the right side of the ship, and ye shall find. They cast
therefore, and now they were not able to draw it for the multitude of fishes. Therefore that
disciple whom Jesus loved saith unto Peter, It is the Lord. . . . As soon then as they were come to
land, they saw a fire of coals there, and fish laid thereon, and bread. . . . Jesus saith unto them,
Come and dine. (John 21:1, 4–7, 9, 12)

MORNING MEAL AT GALILEE

Much of the shoreline of the Sea of Galilee is formed by steep slopes rising directly from the water's edge, and the sea bottom drops sharply from the shoreline out to the central depths. Because of the precipitous pitch of the sea floor, fishermen casting their nets for bottom-feeding fish have long been obliged to position their boats very close to the shore, since the fish move there from the depths of the lake at night.

The fishermen mentioned in the Gospel account had been fishing where and when fish were most likely to be caught: inshore, at night. Thus, when dawn broke, the boat was near enough to shore for a person there to be seen and heard.

And he led them out as far as to Bethany, and he lifted up his hands, and blessed them. And
it came to pass, while he blessed them, he was parted from them, and carried up into heaven.
And they worshipped him, and returned to Jerusalem with great joy. . . .   (Luke 24:50–52)

ASCENSION

The Gospel of Luke concludes with the event which the later Christian community was to call the Ascension.
After Jesus left them, the disciples returned to Jerusalem "with great joy." As long as the memory of
the Ascension was vivid in their hearts, they had little reason to mark its exact geographical location. But by the
fourth century, travelers to Jerusalem were shown a high place at the summit of the Mount of Olives and
told that this was the site of the Ascension. Shortly thereafter a church was built there, only to be destroyed by
the Persians in A.D. 614. It was replaced by a circular church built in such a way that lamps hung at the
opening near the top would allow a perpetual light to burn at the point of the Ascension and at the same time be
visible to the city of Jerusalem across the Kidron Valley. After the Moslem conquest the church was
incorporated, as it may be seen today, within the precincts of a small mosque.

From the high point of the Mount of Olives, Jesus could have seen the places where he had begun
and fulfilled his earthly ministry—the hills of Bethlehem and the city of Jerusalem.

*Heaven
and earth
shall pass away,
but my words
shall not pass
away.*

(Matthew 24:35)